My name is Aunty Nita Taylor and I’m a Gumbaynggirr Elder. I was born in Grafton in the beautiful Northern Rivers of New South Wales. I am one of twelve children and my family name is Duroux. This is a well-known Indigenous name in the Clarence Valley.

As a young girl, I lived in a place called Cangai. This small town is in the foothills of the Gibraltar Range, which is part of the Great Dividing Range. This range stretches from the very top to the very bottom of Australia.

Cangai is over seventy kilometres from Grafton, and it took us over an hour to travel there by car. Back when I was a little girl, we didn't own a car and if we wanted to go anywhere, we had to walk.

When we went into town, we had to travel with the mail truck. The mail truck also collected the milk cans, and we had to sit in the back with them. The roads were dirt and by the time we got to town, we were covered in dust!

The house we lived in had four bedrooms. It was very old and made of timber and sat on top of a hill. The kitchen was separated from the rest of the house and the toilet was also out the back. We had no electricity or running water in the house.

New House

There was a creek at the bottom of the hill. When we needed water, we would have to walk down to the creek and carry the water all the way up the hill. We would use the water for drinking and washing dishes. The water in the creek was running and that's where we used to swim and wash ourselves. It was so deep that as a child, if you stood in the middle, the water would be well over your head.

The Mann River was further away and it used to take us a long time to walk there. We never needed to carry any food with us because there would always be plenty of fruit to pick off the trees and vines along the way. We had our choice of lemons, oranges, mandarins, strawberries, raspberries, gooseberries and passionfruit. We never went hungry!

We would stay all day, fishing for fish and turtles. We used hand lines to catch fish and my brothers would dive deep under the water for the turtles.

Dad used to sometimes pan for gold in the Mann River. It was a popular river for gold panning, and there was even a gold mine nearby. The Mann River is a very important river and it flows into an even larger river called the Clarence River. The towns of Grafton and South Grafton were built around the Clarence River. Locals call it the Mighty Clarence because it's one of the largest and most important rivers in Australia!

We had plenty of great, rolling hills around the house and we used to have fun sliding down them on a flattened cardboard box. We also used to build paper boats and follow them along the creek as they floated along. If we didn't have paper, we would use sticks instead. We used to have so much fun racing them along the creek.

Further along the creek, there was a lovely, rocky place which was nice and cool and shady. Lots of moss and pretty wildflowers grew in this area. We would build our dolls' house on the rocks amongst the moss and the flowers and use sticks for people. We didn't have much when we were young, but we always managed to make our own fun and loved growing up in this beautiful part of Australia.

Word bank

- Gumbaynggirr
- Duroux
- Indigenous
- Clarence River
- Cangai
- Gibraltar
- Dividing
- Australia
- kilometres
- separated
- electricity
- ourselves
- Mann River
- mandarins
- strawberries
- raspberries
- gooseberries
- passionfruit
- popular
- cardboard